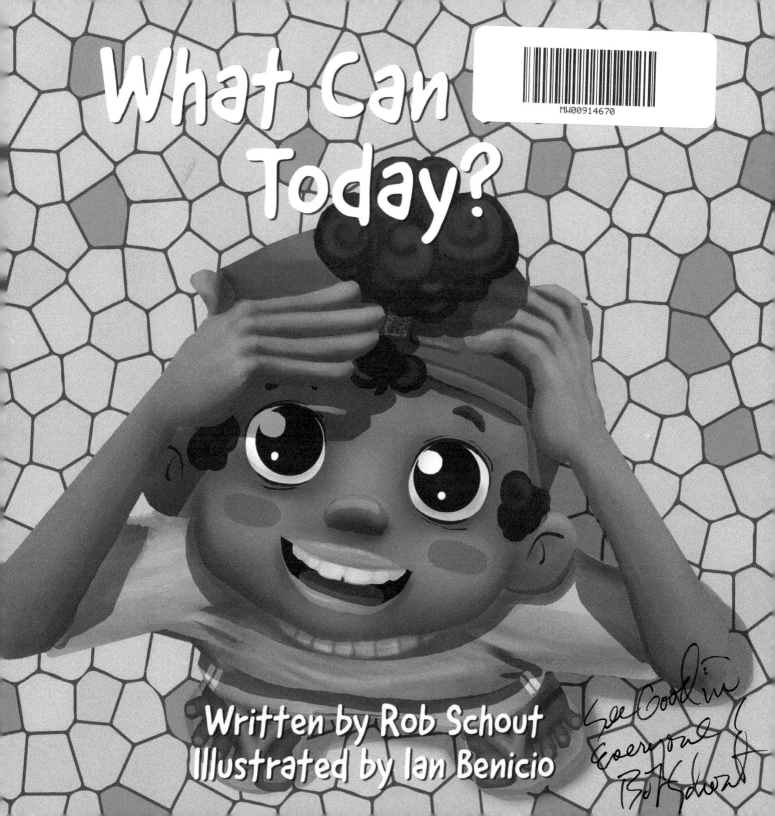

What Can Today?

Written by Rob Schout
Illustrated by Ian Benicio

As I awake...

I look in the mirror
and gaze at ME,
and imagine the day
that is about to be.

With my mind
wide open and
full of glee,
I can't wait to
discover what I
can see.

I look around at the world outside.
Everything's there, nothing to hide.

I see a world full of
goodness, color, and life,
and not of hardship,
struggle, and strife.

I see a world full
of hope, acceptance,
and love;
A world that I'm a super
important part of.

I'm off to school, then off to play,
oh, the things that I'll see today.

I can see planes and birds that fly so high, and fluffy white clouds that dance in the sky.

I can see trees and
flowers,
their colors so bright,
and all around me,
I see sunlight.

I see happiness and joy as I skip along,
and rocks and stones singing their song.

The wonders of life spring
and abound,
with every sight and
every sound.

I see happiness filling every person's heart.
Each person is like a work of art.

I see people who could use a neighbor and friend,
In me they can trust and always depend.

I see chances to help
people in need,
and chances to do lots of
good deeds.

But never forget to look and see,
the good inside you, and the good inside me.

Dedication/Gratitude

Dedication

To all the children of the world, make yourself seen. Each of you is important and can change this world for good. See the beauty within yourself. See the goodness and beauty in all people, cultures, animals, and plants around the world. Thank you for seeing the many ways you can make a difference.

Gratitude

Leandro Barros Viana, thank you, from the wholeness of my heart, for helping me see the many wonders that each day has to offer, right before our eyes and in every culture and corner of the world. You're a constant reminder to simply open my eyes and see the incredible beauty in the smallest of creatures and the grandest expanses.

Message from the Author

This book is part of the I CAN series. Each book offers children an invitation to Do, Say, See, and Give from the love inside them every day!

Well-intentioned teachers, guardians, and mentors sometimes plant the seeds of limiting beliefs in children's minds — "there's nothing you can do," "life is always hard," "you're not good." These seeds often grow with the child into sadness, limitation, shame, or fear.

But the I CAN books convey messages of empowerment toward love, kindness, and compassion — for both children and adults. It's up to me, to you, and to us to Do, Say, See, and Give each day to make this planet a better, kinder, more loving world.

You can also visit schoutitout.com to download supplementary activity booklets with coloring pages, mazes, word search puzzles, and reflection questions for both children and adults to enjoy.

Thank you for being a part of the I CAN family!

Peace always,
Rob Schout

About the Author

Rob Schout is an author, poet, life skills educator, management trainer, professional and personal life coach, and international business consultant. Whew! That's a lot! He believes in pursuing every dream and living on purpose in life.

Rob's voice and energy fill a room, and his provocative positivity inspires children and adults alike. He believes there is an innate goodness in every person, solutions to every dilemma, and pathways to every dream. The key to unleashing it all is in the choices we make and the actions we take.

That's what the I CAN books are all about. They help children realize they can make choices and take action each day to bring about more good in the world by what they choose to say, do, give, and be each day.

About the Illustrator

Ian Benicio is an artist and a father. He has a bachelor's degree in Data Processing, but what fulfills him is to translate dreams and fantasies into art that offers a good experience.

What else can you SEE today?

What Can I Do Today?

Inspire a child to bring more goodness into the world today! Follow a little girl's journey of curiosity as she contemplates all the things she can do to help people have a better day.

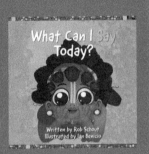

What Can I Say Today?

Encourage a child to speak words of love to others today. Join a boisterous young girl who has so much to say as she goes through her day. Wonder with her about all the words she can use to help others smile and take away sadness.

What Can I Give Today?

Open a child's heart to the joy of giving today. Follow a little girl's fun-filled journey through a day as she ponders all the things she has been given and the many things she can give to others to bring happiness and joy to the world each day.

Discover the entire I CAN series and download interactive games and grown-up questions to help continue the conversation with your children – www.schoutitout.com

CPSIA information can be obtained
at www.ICGtesting.com
Printed in the USA
JSHW040401270723
45461JS00007B/160